NOW

Refuse to let the moment pass.

NOW

Refuse to let the moment pass.

Delme Linscott

NOW

Self - Published in February 2010
www.LivingInGrace.co.za
Text: © Delme Linscott
Editing by Wesley Church Team

All Scripture quotations, unless otherwise indicated, are taken from the HOLY BIBLE, NEW INTERNATIONAL VERSION, copyright 1973, 1978, 1984 International Bible Society. Used by permission of Zondervan Bible Publishers.

Scripture quotations marked 'Message' (MSG) are taken from THE MESSAGE. Copyright © by Eugene H Petersen, 1993, 1994, 1995. Used by permission of NavPress Publishing Group.

Scripture quotations marked NLT are taken from the HOLY BIBLE, NEW LIVING TRANSLATION, copyright © 1996. Used by permission of Tyndale House Publishers, Inc.,
Wheaton, Illinois 60189. All rights reserved.

Cover design: Paul de Villiers and Delme Linscott
Cover image supplied by iStockphoto.com

ISBN 978-0-620-46248-8

Dedication

For Kim, Declan, Nathan and Joshua –
you all mean the world to me.
The words of this book have changed the way I live and I pray
that I would not let any moment pass us by.

In memory of my cousin, Christopher 'Kit' Edwards & my
friend, Barry Marshall.

"Carpe Diem! Seize the day.
Make your lives extraordinary."
- **Dead Poets Society**

CONTENTS

"Twenty years from now you will be more disappointed by the things that you didn't do than by the ones you did do. So throw off the bowlines. Sail away from the safe harbour. Catch the trade winds in your sails. Explore. Dream. Discover."
– **Mark Twain**

A NOTE FROM THE AUTHOR

To you the reader –thank you for taking the time to read these pages. Before you continue I need to mention a few things:

This was not the book I had intended to write next – that copy is still on my 'to do' list. However, life doesn't always work out the way we plan and so through a combination of circumstances and in a short space of time, *Now* was written.

In order for this final product to end up in your hands, there were a number of fantastic friends who helped in incredible ways. Every one of these people believed enough in this book to sacrifice their precious time. I am humbled by their support and generosity.

Kim Linscott – thanks for graciously believing in my ideas and helping me shape the initial ideas of the book.
Paul De Villiers - for your help with the awesome cover, the website and good coffee!

Tyron Bache – for your creative gift in crafting the website and for your amazing input and encouragement.

Gareth Killeen – for your friendship and agreeing to write the foreword.

Andy and Gareth – I will remember that day and plane trip forever. Thank you.

Xavier – thanks for inspiring me to believe that things are possible! Keep pursuing your dream my friend.

Stuart, Ann, Izzy, Jenny, Tony, Kim, David – Thank you for your help in editing the content and for being patient with my shocking punctuation. I am grateful for all of your thoughts and insights. Your words have added excellence to the finished product.

Quin, Mike and Mark – thanks for your support and willingness to help in any way.

To my family – for always believing in me and for encouraging me to reach for my dreams.

To my friends in the various Churches I have served – it is a privilege to be your friend and pastor.

To Jesus Christ – I owe you everything. You are my friend, my inspiration and my Saviour.

FOREWORD

In Delme's first book, *Living Oceans Apart*, he addressed a subject that touches the lives of everyone who struggles with the pain of living great distances away from loved ones. It proved to be an important message of hope and encouragement for many.

This second book that Delme has authored, however, is perhaps even more powerful because its message is directly relevant to *every* human being. Seize the day! Live in the now! Live to the full!

Delme freely admits there is nothing new about these messages at all, yet at the same time they are both timeless and priceless. Timeless, because the tendency to thoughtlessly waste our precious God-given moments of life is sadly a universal weakness clearly evident throughout human history, and thus, requires continual challenge. Priceless, because the immense value of hearing and heeding this particular message just cannot be measured, it can only be seen, tasted, touched and experienced in the quality of relational and personal fruit it will inevitably bear.

Yet, the essence of this message, while easy enough to grasp proves far more difficult to hold onto for any length of time, which again, is exactly why the lessons and truths touched upon in this book are ones that we need to be reminded of repeatedly.

Delme has taken up the challenge to help us remember that every moment counts and he has produced a book which I believe will prove to be an absolute treasure-trove of inspiration for many.

Delme has a strongly personal and pastoral style of writing that manages to not only convey his message but also carry it home to the heart. Delme shares that the writing of this book was inspired by the tragic passing of a very dear mutual friend (the Rev. Barry Marshall), and somehow the deep emotions evoked in him by this event are carried through in his words. This infuses the overall message with a passion and urgency that proves difficult to resist.

All this and more is why I voraciously devoured this book, and it is why I will be buying extra copies and handing them out to various loved ones, because I so want them to hear and heed its message. It is also exactly why I am encouraging you to not only carefully read this important book but also act upon it. Now!

Rev. Gareth Killeen

Chapter 1

INTRODUCTION

"The tragedy of life is not that it ends so soon, but that we wait so long to begin it." – **W. M. Lewis**

"Over and over again, we lose sight of what is important and what isn't." – **Epictetus**

I have started to write this short book at the end of an emotional week. It has been just a few days since we said goodbye to a friend of mine, who died in very tragic circumstances. His death has shocked me and left me doing a lot of soul-searching.

This isn't the place to throw my plethora of unanswered questions into an atmosphere of doubt and faith, but his death has certainly woken me from a lethargic sleep – I now want to seize every waking moment as a gift from God. He inspired me in his life, and even in his untimely death he has now propelled me into action. As a result of all of this, my family have been the beneficiaries of extra hugs, more quality time, new spontaneity and a desire to revolutionize my approach to life.

The concept of 'making every moment count' is not new - we have heard it many times before. However, it becomes fresh and dynamic when we are confronted with the fragility of life or when we are moved by some life-changing experience. Deep emotions stir within us as we grasp the eternal perspectives within the frailty of our existence.

The well-known Latin phrase, *Carpe Diem* (commonly translated as 'Seize the Day') speaks about gathering every opportunity we can or doing what we can, before it is too late. Roman poet Horace used the following phrase in a verse from his poem, *Odes 1.11*: '*Carpe diem quam minimum credula postero.*' When translated these words read, "Seize the day, trusting as little as possible in the future." In a nutshell, the ideas that follow in this short book explore this concept of seizing every moment!

For me, life boils down to this one statement – "every moment is a gift from God." Every breath we breathe will never be captured or exhaled again. Every waking hour holds enormous potential and opportunities for us. The future lies only a fraction of a second before us, yet we still can't trust in that future. We may not get to enjoy it. We can only be certain of this moment, this breath, this heartbeat.

Working alongside people in a Christian community, I have the privilege of engaging in all aspects of their lives – and even in their deaths. Every memorial service or funeral I lead moves me immensely. Without fail I end up reflecting on my own life as I drive home after the service. I now see these opportunities as unique gifts. It may seem strange, but as these moments are presented to me, without my asking for them, I get to re-evaluate the life I am blessed to live. So, just as one beloved person leaves this life, I am forced to embrace my own mortality. Then I desperately strive to 'seize the day' and to live life to the full.

But what about you? Do you find yourself wanting to make every moment count, but don't even know where to start? Do your good intentions never materialise into anything significant? Do you feel as if your life is racing by and you are not sure whether you are actually making any difference at all?

If any of these thoughts have crossed your mind, know that you are in good company. I am your new best friend! However, even though there are other people who struggle with the same things as you do (as reassuring as that may be), life doesn't stop passing by. We are still left with unique moments to catch and opportunities to seize.

This short book is just a beginning for us. It could be a springboard to a life of appreciating all that we have and every second of our existence. If you find anything inspiring from these pages then take it, use it and let it motivate you. All I ask is this:

Don't just sit there and let your life go to waste! You were created for more than that.

Living in Grace,
Delme

Chapter 2

19

SAY IT NOW

"I can live for two months on a good compliment." - **Mark Twain**

"Be who you are and say what you feel because those who mind don't matter and those who matter don't mind." – **Dr Seuss**

I have encountered a number of people who have been disappointed by hurtful comments and ill-timed words. A lot of these people have regretted the manner in which they have reacted, longing to take back words that wounded others deeply. Sadly, no spoken word ever has the chance to be taken back. The words we speak echo into the chamber of life and ultimately leave ripples in the pool of humanity.

However, I have also counselled a number of people who have felt guilty at never saying what they wanted to say. Sydney J. Harris points out that "regret for the things we did can be tempered by time; it is regret for the things we did not do that is inconsolable." Missed opportunities are exactly that – missed, lost, tragic! How many times have we wanted to say something but just never got around to it? Time passes, people move away or die unexpectedly and then we live with this deep sense of regret. Why didn't we say what we needed to say?

In *No Compromise: The Life Story of Keith Green*, Melody Green recounts the last conversation she had with her husband, Keith, just before he left for the airport. He was due to catch a flight for a proposed mission trip. With an eerie sense of foreboding Keith called out to her as his car pulled out of the driveway: "If I don't come back, raise Rebekah to be a woman of God."

Melody, who was pregnant with their fourth child, replied: "What about this one?", patting her stomach.

Keith retorted, "If it's a boy, name him Daniel!"

Melody joked back, "You mean you don't want me to name him after you?"

Keith said, "Okay. If it's a boy, you can name him after me."

With that he drove off and those were the last words Keith spoke to Melody. Within a few minutes Melody heard the news that Keith's plane had crashed, killing him instantly along with their two oldest children, Josiah (3) and Bethany (2). Melody was left as a widow to raise Rebekah (1) and a few months later, Rachel.

If we were in Melody's situation, what would we have wanted to say to our loved ones? Would we have said it?

In his book *Life Focus*, Jerry Foster asks this unusual question:

"Do you hope that friends and co-workers who attend your memorial service are filled with gratitude for your contribution to their lives?"

This is a deeply thought-provoking question and there are few of us who wouldn't want this to be true of our lives. In reality, I believe that many human beings subconsciously long for these three things:

ɛɔ We desire to be loved and appreciated.

ɛɔ We want to leave some legacy.

ɛɔ We seek to make our lives count - to live a significant and memorable life.

Whilst, there is nothing wrong with these desires (they are actually quite remarkable things to strive for) there is perhaps a more profound thought for us to consider. Should we not turn these goals around and ask this question?

Are we willing to turn our own desires into fulfilling somebody else's deepest longings?

Let me explain what I mean. If we desire some of the things I have just mentioned, to be fulfilled in our own lives, then there is a great probability that many other people want the same things we do. Yet, in a sense, we hold the key to fulfilling these desires in the lives of others. We have the power to influence other people's lives, by responding to their deepest longings and their greatest needs.

So, how do we even begin to do something as radical as what I am suggesting? Well, the answer is summarised in three simple words…

Say it now!

We can start changing the lives of others by applying this simple concept of telling people what they mean to us and how their lives have impacted on our lives. We can encourage them with the power of words! Mother Teresa pointed out that "kind words can be short and easy to speak, but their echoes are truly endless." We can 'say it now' and allow those words to touch the lives of someone else.

At some of the memorial services that I have attended, I have been privileged to hear many stirring tributes and heartfelt eulogies. On numerous occasions, I have found myself thinking, "I wonder if this person knew all of these things? Did they know how much of a difference they made in the lives of these people who are now mourning?" Sadly, a few times I am left with the empty feeling that they were probably not aware of their powerful impact. Perhaps they knew that they were loved, but to what extent?

Seizing every moment means that we need to tell people how much they mean to us – and we need to speak these words now! David Brin agrees with this sentiment when he writes, "Why must conversions always come so late? Why do people always apologize to corpses?" I am baffled as to why we wait until people we love, admire and respect die before we say remarkable things about them? They can't hear their own eulogies. They can't read their gravestones. They can't see all the moving tributes on Facebook. So, why don't we tell them now?

Can you imagine if all of these people had heard these inspiring words whilst they were alive – imagine the impact on their lives! I dream of what our world could become, if people knew without a doubt that they were appreciated and loved; and moreover if every man, woman and child knew that they were loved not only by someone else, but also loved by a truly immense God. Surely we would all be spurred onto greater things in life and perhaps we would then begin to see unprecedented miracles.

Perhaps the apostle Paul grasped some of this awe when he wrote these words:

> *"No eye has seen,*
> *No ear has heard,*
> *No mind can know,*
> *What God has in store for those who love him."*
> – **1 Corinthians 2:9**

When people know that they are loved by God and by others, it can be a powerful catalyst towards a revolution of change. Can you dream of being part of this change? I can.

In his brilliant work *Carpe Manana*, Leonard Sweet shares this imaginary encounter between a patient and his doctor:

A man went to his doctor for a check-up and after a while the doctor told him the bad news. "You only have a short time to live."

"How long?" the man wanted to know.

"Ten..." replied the doctor.

"Ten what?" the man asked. "Ten years? Ten months? Ten weeks? Ten days? Ten what?"

The doctor replied, "Ten, nine, eight, seven ..."

Whilst this story may be only fictional, it does convey a powerful truth. Time is ticking, time is short. If you have something to say to people that is significant, say it now. In fact, we should have said it yesterday. Even as we have read this paragraph we have just lost another 10 seconds.

A few years ago, Mike and the Mechanics wrote a very moving song, entitled, *The Living Years*. The words were inspired by a broken relationship between B.A. Robertson and his father. Every time I hear the words from the song, I think about the important people in my life and pray that I don't ever take them for granted. The following words from the song can leave an indelible impact on one's spirit:

> *I just wish I could have told him*
> *In the living years...*
> *Crumpled bits of paper*
> *Filled with imperfect thought*

Stilted conversations
I'm afraid that's all we've got.

I wasn't there that morning
When my father passed away
I didn't get to tell him
All the things I had to say.

Say it loud, say it clear
You can listen as well as you hear
It's too late when we die
To admit we don't see eye to eye.

As we move from this concept of 'saying it now' let us take these words from C. Morley to heart:

"If we discovered that we had five minutes left to say all we wanted to say, every telephone booth would be occupied by people calling other people to stammer that they love them. Why wait until the last five minutes?"

Reflection:

1. If you could *'say it now'* to anyone in your family or circle of friends, who would it be?

2. What would you tell them?

3. Consider this quote:

"The two worst strategic mistakes to make are acting prematurely and letting an opportunity slip." - **Paul Coelho**

www.livingingrace.co.za

Chapter 3

BE FULLY PRESENT - LIVE IN THE NOW

"I never wear a watch, because I always know it is *now* – and *now* is when you should do it." –
Steve Mariucci

"Do it now.
Do whatever you can do right now." –
Thomas à Kempis

It happened to me again today, whilst I was spending some time with my kids before my evening meetings. They were asking me to play a few games with them and I joined in, but sadly my mind was elsewhere. I played the games with them, but I was busy thinking about the meeting later on, as well all kinds of other commitments and people. I felt guilty. I felt like a cheat. I was present in the flesh, but my spirit was miles away.

How do we live fully in the moment? In our modern world of constant busyness, social networking and diverse responsibilities, how do we enjoy every moment? It's quite hard, isn't it, or perhaps it's just me?

Without moving too much into the field of philosophy or other religious thought, choosing to 'live in the now' is something that affects every human being. We all struggle with appreciating the essence of every second of life.

Most of us want to embrace the abundant life given to us by God and to make our lives count for Christ. We also want to honour our families with every part of our beings – and that includes our minds and spirits, as well as our bodies. I don't feel that it is sufficient for my children only to *see* my physical presence - they have the right to my entire being – fully present and focused.

The English author, Margaret Storm Jameson, also has some advice for us on this matter. She once expressed the view that we all spend too much time living in the past, feeling regret for lost joys or shame for things badly done. Even when our minds turn to the future, we spend an inordinate amount of time longing for it or dreading it. "The only way to live," she said, "is to accept each minute as an unrepeatable miracle . . .

Work at your work. Play at your play. Shed your tears. Enjoy your laughter. Now is the time of your life."

We make a lot of jokes about the fact that men struggle to multi-task, but men can actually do more than one thing at a time. Look at me right now – I am thinking, breathing and writing at the same time – I hope you are impressed! Yet, jokes aside, multi-tasking could be the enemy of living fully in 'the now.'

For me, if I am trying to do more than one thing at a time, there is a greater chance that I will be more focused on one than on the rest. Yes, I can watch Television, while typing a text message and chatting with my wife. I can do these all simultaneously, but only one of the three will get my fullest attention.

What is getting your fullest attention today and is it being a blessing in your life?

I love this quote from Henry David Thoreau, which was also used in *Dead Poets Society*:

"I went to the woods because I wanted to live deliberately, I wanted to live deep and suck out all the marrow of life, to put to rout all that was not life and not when I had come to die discover that I had not lived."

There is something intentional in these words; something that speaks of making deliberate decisions while we can. For the majority of us, we are confident that today will not be our last day (or at least we pray it won't be). So immediately we lose some of the intensity of living fully in the present. Sadly, this means that we probably won't do something about it – we will carry on living with the view of a perpetual tomorrow.

Sergio Milandr challenges us to think more of how our lives are being played out in the present. For him, there is a responsibility to choose to love *now*, as it has a ripple effect on our community. He writes:

> "The one command Jesus left us with is that we love God, our neighbour and ourselves. But are we, in fact, doing that at the moment? Or are we saying, we'll love tomorrow, we're too tired today? Love is something that only happens in the present. If I am not loving now, I certainly won't be loving tomorrow. Love either is or it isn't. The person I am is either a loving person or not a loving person and it's *now* that I need to be loving."

This is a powerful challenge for me and yet it is not the first time I have heard these words. Jesus has been inviting us to 'love another' (John 13:34) for close on two thousand years and we have still not been able to do that fully as yet. We may have the best intentions to do this 'one day', but that continues to be an unknown date in the future, unless we choose to love now.

By the way, I have discovered that my kids know when I am not fully present with them. Kids are intuitive – they are switched on and they will say it like it is. They know how to keep me grounded. When I play with them now, they tell me to put my cell phone down and to play with them! That means doing it NOW – it means that I need to choose not to stand around alongside them, but to actually play with them.

In 2008, rock band Nickelback wrote a song entitled, *If Today Was Your Last Day?* I never thought that I would be looking for fundamental truth in the lyrics of a rock group, but these words are certainly very apt:

If today was your last day, and tomorrow
was too late
Could you say goodbye to yesterday?
Would you live each moment like your last?
Leave old pictures in the past
Donate every dime you have?
If today was your last day?

We finish this chapter, with these inspirational words:

"God asks no man whether he will accept life. That is not the choice. You must take it. The only question is how." - **Henry Ward Beecher**

Reflection:

1. When you multi-task, who or what gets the most focus?

2. If our answer to this question is an object instead of a person then perhaps we need to begin redefining our priorities.

3. What is the hardest part of 'living in the now' for you?

4. Read John 13:34 again. Read it in a few different translations and see what God could be saying to you.

Chapter 4

37

MAKE DREAMS BECOME REALITY

"For my part I know nothing with any certainty, but
the sight of the stars makes me dream."
- Vincent van Gogh

"I want the whole Christ for my Saviour, the whole
Bible for my book, the whole Church for my
fellowship, and the
whole world for my mission field."
- John Wesley

$\mathbf{T}$hese words of John Wesley may sound like a far-fetched dream. They may even seem arrogant to some, but this never stopped him from reaching for it! He wanted to glorify God with his hopes and dreams. If there was a human element in his dreams then John Wesley would have been the first to correct his pride. Wesley knew that in order for the world to know about the love of Jesus, ordinary men and women needed to dream risky dreams.

Dale Carnegie echoes this sentiment when he says: "The person who goes the farthest is generally the one who is willing to do and dare. The sure-thing boat never gets far from the shore." There are far too many of us who are living our lives 'playing it safe' – we choose the easy options and yet, in the end, this only serves to become a source of frustration for us.

Jerry Foster speaks about a concept called the 'Vector Principle' in *Life on Purpose*. He describes it as follows: "Achieving a desired outcome in your life is the result of consistently making positive choices that vector you toward that outcome."

For those of us who don't understand vectors, what he simply means is this:
If we want to make a big dream become a reality (sometime in the future) we have to start doing small things, or making small decisions, now. Even a small thing done today, can increase the likelihood of our achieving this immense dream later.

I suppose we could compare it with space travel. If a rocket is positioned only a fraction of a degree out from its perfect setting then, when it is launched into space, it could potentially veer a great distance from its destination. Small mistakes made today can increase exponentially in the future.

Conversely though, if we start with a tiny action today, this could have a huge effect later on in our lives. A miniscule change today could translate into the realisation of a substantial dream tomorrow.

So what dreams do you have at the moment? Why are we so often afraid to speak of these dreams? Do we feel that people will judge us? Or is it perhaps easier not to speak of them, fearing being held accountable to them? This book is an example of this. I wanted to find a way of getting people to 'seize the day' and to appreciate one another. I held the idea in my mind for a while, nurturing it and not speaking about it. This was a safe option. As soon as I told Kim and a friend what I planned to do, then my dreams were out there waiting to be scrutinized and potentially to be scoffed at.

However, it is also an immense privilege to have people encourage you to fulfil these same dreams. More often than not, people see the unique potential in your dream and through their encouragement we are spurred on to greater things.

Gutzon Borglum had a remarkable dream. In 1924 he was brave enough to share his dream with the world. Looking at the Black Hills of South Dakota, Gutzon proclaimed, "American history shall march along that skyline." Three years later Borglum began sculpting the images of George Washington, Abraham Lincoln, Thomas Jefferson and Theodore Roosevelt on the granite face of the 2000 meter Mount Rushmore. Most of the sculpting was done by experienced miners under Borglum's direction. Working with jackhammers and dynamite, they removed over 400 000 tons of outer rock, cutting within 7 centimeters of the final surface. When Gutzon died in March 1941, his dream of the world's biggest sculpture was near completion. His son Lincoln finished the work that October, some 14 years after it first began.

When you gaze out into our world, do you see only a mountain of rock or do you envision something remarkable that can take shape through your life and the power of God's hand? Anatole France wrote,

"To accomplish great things, we must not only act, but also dream; not only plan, but also believe."

Michael Johnson was another young man who had a dream and at the turn of the 21st century, the world had the privilege of watching his dream come to life. When Olympic sprint champion, Michael Johnson, ran in a 200 or 400 metre event, crowds erupted with applause and excitement. We were all in awe of his ability as an athlete.

However, as millions of fans appreciated his victories, few of us realised that his moments of fame had first taken root in his own dreams. For over ten years he trained, dreamed and focused on his final goals. In an interview Johnson once said: "I crafted a decade of dreams into ambitions, ambitions into goals, and finally hammered my goals into plans."

Reflecting on Michael Johnson's success, present Springbok Sevens Coach, Paul Treu, commented: "Michael Johnson succeeded in the race because he had succeeded before the race."[i] Those are powerful words. They should encourage us to dream, to hope, to plan. The person who has no dreams is bound to feel hopelessness towards life. We all have the ability to dream!

The writer of Proverbs says it like this: *"Where there is no vision, the people perish."*

God wants us to dream big dreams and to plan to succeed for *His Glory*. I write these words in italics, because sometimes we confuse our own egos with God's sovereign plan. If John Wesley had served God faithfully only in his community, and the world had not become his parish, then Wesley would have accepted that. But he was ready to work alongside God in dreaming a big dream. He expected that his God was a miraculous God and so he lived as though he was able to achieve all things.

There is a powerful Rabbinic saying that says, "Everyone must carry two pieces of paper with him and look at them every day. On one it is written: 'You are as dust and ashes.' And on the other: 'For you the universe was created.'" This reminds us that our lives are so finely tied into the grace of our Creator, that we need to constantly remember that we are 'but a breath,' yet God has given us the entire universe as our home. This is all a sober reminder of our smallness, but also of our incredible ability to change the world.

Lastly, how would you respond to this question?

"If money were no object, what career would you be pursuing right now?"

I am amazed at some of the responses to this question. There are very few people who admit that they would be in the same career and perhaps even in the same city. This is a sad reality that millions of people wake up to every morning – their dreams have not materialised and for some, their dreams have turned into a nightmare. Tantalisingly close, but yet they remain just out of reach.

In order to fully reflect on this chapter, I encourage you to spend a few minutes responding to these five questions.

Reflection:

1. What dream have you held within your heart for many years?

2. What stumbling blocks are preventing you from fulfilling your dreams?

3. Would God be glorified through your dream? If you answered 'yes' to this question, then why don't you ask God to help you fulfil your dream.

4.   Pray and reflect on this quote:

"There is nothing like a dream to create the future."
                    – **Victor Hugo**

Chapter 5

OVERCOME YOUR FEARS

"Don't waste life in doubts and fears." – **Ralph Waldo Emerson**

"Too many of us are not living our dreams because we are living our fears."
– Les Brown

At the end of the previous chapter I asked a question about our dreams. If we had to ask people what is stopping them from fulfilling their dreams a fair number of them would respond with things like:

- Responsibilities
- Finances
- Lack of opportunity
- Family
- Lack of skills
- Past disappointments

While not denying that many of these issues do present real challenges to fulfilling any dream, it is sad that we often aren't willing to be honest about the biggest stumbling block to fulfilling our dreams. This obstacle is summed up as the 'F-word'. Yes, I am talking about FEAR. Fear of failure, fear of rejection, fear of learning – all kinds of fears loom large before us, potentially destroying any chance we may have had of reaching for our dreams.

The topic of fear is well documented and it has been argued that there are five fears common to most humans. These are the fear of poverty, being alone, illness, old age and death. Any of these fears is understandable, but it is important to identify which of these could potentially be destructive. In the end, I believe that fear is a raw emotion that wells up within our hearts and threatens to derail us from living abundant lives.

In contrast to the reality of 'genuine' fear, millions of people live daily with phobias, which have been described as 'irrational fears'. For example, people struggle with agoraphobia (fear of open spaces), acrophobia (fear of heights) and arachnophobia (fear of spiders).

Apparently a number of women suffer from rhytiphobia (fear of wrinkles) and a few men with peladophobia(fear of losing their hair), but there are millions of people who suffer daily from 'what-if-phobia.' (If you never knew this phobia existed, then now you do. It is the fear of "what if?") It normally comes in the form of questions, such as these:

What if I fail?
What if I say the wrong thing?
What if they don't like me?
What if my idea doesn't work?

'What-if-phobia' strikes at the heart of our emotions and leaves many people paralysed with fear. The saddest result of this phobia is that many books are left unwritten, stories left untold, inventions never created and love never found.

The well-documented story of Thomas Edison's life highlights the number of times he failed in his attempts at inventing the light bulb – he failed over one thousand times. That is a lot of failures, don't you think?
When would you have given up - after 10, 40, 100 or 200 attempts?
Edison believed so strongly in his goal and dream that he persevered until it became a reality. The world will be forever grateful for Thomas' dogged determination. In our day and age it is hard to fathom life without the electric light.

Some pessimists point out that someone else would have invented light bulbs, even if Mr Edison had given up and the pessimists may well be right. However, this never happened. We would have forgiven Edison for wanting to give up, but he didn't. He never let the fear of 'what if?' stop him from fulfilling his dreams.

There are a number of Biblical characters who inspire me, but David and Simon Peter stand out among the rest as the most intriguing and inspirational. If I could ask David and Simon Peter each a question, it would have to be these:

To David…
When did you overcome your fear of giants?
To Simon Peter…
When did you overcome your fear of walking on water?

What I would like to know is: did David only overcome his fear of big hairy men when he saw Goliath lying at his feet? More than likely not! I guess that it was about the same time that he overcame his fear of lions and other wild animals, which was probably at the same time he truly understood how powerful God was!

And what about Simon Peter? Well, I don't think he really overcame this fear of walking on water, but what he realised was that fear was nothing in comparison with Jesus. After all it was Jesus who called him to walk on the water, so in that moment Peter chose to leave his fears behind. Perhaps this is why George Macdonald wrote, "The first thing in all progress is to leave something behind." Peter progressed, because he left fear behind!

The psalmist recorded his own experience of fear in these words:
"I sought the Lord, and he answered me; he delivered me from all my fears." – Psalm 34:4

In this Psalm we read how he called out to God, seeking answers for the dilemmas he was facing. He intimates that these issues were bogging him down in fear and that he wanted to move beyond this debilitating scenario. For him, the only person who could help him overcome his crisis of fear was the Lord. The words, "he delivered me from my fears" should be good news for the countless number of us paralysed by fear.

So what are you so afraid of? How many 'what-ifs' do you come up with before you are willing to risk something? Perhaps, today is the day you need to bury your 'what-if-phobia' and to allow God to deliver you from your fear. The following story may help you along the way:

Wilma Rudolph was the twentieth of 22 children. She was born prematurely and her survival was doubtful. When she was four, she contracted double pneumonia and scarlet fever, which left her with a paralyzed left leg. At age nine, she removed the metal leg brace she had been dependent on and began to walk without it. By thirteen she had developed a rhythmic walk, which doctors said was a miracle. That same year she decided to become a runner. She entered a race and came in last.

For the next several years, every race she entered, she came in last. Everyone told her to quit, and while that might sound harsh, they had a point. However, she kept on running. Eventually she actually won a race and then another. Soon she was winning every race she entered. In the end, Wilma Rudolph - who was told she would never walk again - went on to win three Olympic gold medals.

That is inspirational!

Reflection:

1. What fears are you facing at the moment?

2. Do you know if other people have conquered these same fears before? IF YES, then what is stopping you from doing the same?

3. How does God respond to our fears?

4. Read 2 Chronicles 20:15-17

"To dare is to lose one's footing momentarily.
To not dare is to lose oneself."
~ **Soren Kierkegaard**

Chapter 6

WHERE TO FROM HERE?

"Time is now measured in seconds." – **Leonard Sweet**

"To change one's life: Start immediately. Do it
flamboyantly.
No exceptions."
– **William James**

A young man from Malawi, William Kamkwamba, is an incredible example of how we can make the most of every moment. His story is told in the moving book, *The Boy Who Harnessed the Wind*. Whereas most people would only be able to see discarded motor parts, old plastic pipes and a discarded bicycle wheel as junk, William saw these pieces of 'junk' as instruments of opportunity.

Growing up in rural Malawi, William faced the daily challenges of poverty and lack of resources. That is except for one major natural resource - wind. Wind is one of the few abundant resources available in Malawi, and the inspired fourteen-year-old saw its energy as a way to power his dreams.

William said, "with a windmill, we'd finally release ourselves from the troubles of darkness and hunger. A windmill meant more than just power, it was freedom." His quest for the abundant life drove William to live out his dreams, no matter the obstacles.

Dave Callanan writes of William: "Despite the biting jeers of village sceptics, young William devoted himself to borrowed textbooks and salvage yards in pursuit of a device that could produce an "electric wind." *The Boy Who Harnessed the Wind* is an inspiring story of an indomitable will that refused to bend to doubt or circumstance. When the world seemed to be against him, William Kamkwamba set out to change it."

We are all like William. We have dreams for a better life. We long for meaningful relationships and a glorious future. Most of us have limited resources and will face constant opposition, yet with God's help we can harness more than the wind – we can harness life itself.

As Bill Hybels said in his final address at the 2009 Leadership Summit, "…your life really matters. This isn't the pre-game [curtain-raiser]. It's *the* game. You have one life to do something that will last for eternity. What are you going to live for? Will it be God's plan?

These are powerful questions for us to answer. So, where do we even begin to get a hold of these penetrating concepts? Perhaps the best place to start is simply to return to the following essential truth, penned by Gene Edwards:

> "The Christian life is, first, having the highest life in you. Secondly, living by means of that life. That makes all other offers taste like sea water."

Jesus emphasised this same sentiment, when he said, "My purpose is to give you life in all its fullness." When we sense that our life has purpose, we begin to glimpse the fullness of God's blessing.

Recently I presided over a memorial service for a remarkable woman who died from post-operative complications. She had lived a good life and had been a blessing to her children, grandchildren and great-grandchildren. What will stick in my memory is how she grasped her own mortality and prior to her operation made up her mind to contact significant people in her life. She wanted to leave nothing to chance and decided to tell others that she loved them. What a powerful example of someone who chose to seize the moment.

I was reading a sermon written by Randy Croft, when I came across this awesome illustration:

> One summer, a man spent the day on the beach in Jacksonville, Florida. The current was unusually strong that day, and more than once, lifeguards jumped down

from their towers to rescue swimmers from the treacherous surf. Finally, the man went to the lifeguard station to express his appreciation for the dedication of these men. When he walked inside, he noticed a sign on the wall in large red letters: "If in doubt, go!" And the man said, "Those same words should be on the walls of every church and on the wall of every person's soul."

Those of us who are willing to risk nothing, will actually risk losing everything. I hope that these final thoughts from Moses will inspire us to be proactive in our decisions:

"Choose Life. Just do it!" – Deuteronomy 30:19 (The Message)

Reflection:

Stephen Levine asks this challenging question:

> "If you were going to die soon and had only one phone
> call you could make, who would you call and what
> would you say? And why are you waiting?"

So why are we waiting?

What are we waiting for?

If you are waiting for someone else to be proactive, then you
may wait forever. You are the one reading these words – you
are the one who is passionate about living in the present.

Why don't you take up the challenge and 'Seize the Day?'

Chapter 7

REFUSE TO LET THIS MOMENT PASS!

"You will never know how much you believe something until it is a matter of life and death."
– **C.S. Lewis**

"A life purpose needs to be greater than we are; something that will outlive us."
- **Jerry Foster**

In October 1972, a flight from Uruguay to Chile crashed into the Andes. Nando Parrado was one of the few survivors of the plane crash, but sadly many of his rugby team-mates, as well as his mother and sister perished in the accident. His ordeal continued when the survivors had to wait 72 days before they were rescued.

Reflecting on his miraculous survival, Nando wrote these words:

> "I was granted a second chance to live. It was not the life I wanted or expected, but I understood that it was my duty *now to live that life* as richly and as hopefully as I could. I vowed to try. I would live with passion and curiosity. I would open myself up to the possibilities of life. I would savour every moment and I would try, every day, to become more human and more alive."

Would it not be intriguing if more of us chose to live our lives "with passion and curiosity", refusing to let any moment pass? This is what God urges us to do - to comprehend that our lives are short, but that we can make them count, regardless of our circumstances. Peter wrote:

> "Since everything here *today* might well be gone tomorrow, do you see how essential it is to live a holy life? Daily expect the 'Day of God', eager for its arrival." - **2 Peter 3:11** (MSG)

Towards the end of his purposeful life, a tired and frail John Wesley got up to preach his last sermon. One would have forgiven him for preaching on a well-known passage such as 2 Timothy 4:7: "I have finished the race. I have fought the good fight." However, staying true to his evangelical roots, Wesley turned to the following scripture passage:

"Seek the Lord while He may be found, call upon Him while He is near" - **Isaiah 55:6**

John Wesley understood that life was short and that we should make use of every chance we get to embrace the love of God. Although he had lived for almost 88 years, he knew that life was a mist – here for a moment and then gone the next.

There are more voices that call out to us from the pages of scripture. They too echo the Creator's call for us to live godly and purposeful lives. These voices remind us of the urgency of living in the 'Now.' Reflecting on the mystery of life and its brevity, James wrote:

"Look here, you people who say, 'Today or tomorrow we are going to a certain town and will stay there a year. We will do business there and make a profit.' How do you know what will happen tomorrow? For your life is like the morning fog – it's here a little while, then it's gone. What you ought to say is, 'If the Lord wants us to, we will live and do this or that.'" – James 4:13-15 (NLT)

It is not just the words of scripture that call us to live every day with purpose and meaning. A number of musicians have echoed this sacred calling, in their mainstream lyrics. Earlier on in chapter three I quoted the chorus from *If Today Was Your Last Day*, written by Nickelback. However, the words from the verse of that song are also relevant and worth reading. My hope is that they would move us to respond in some way.

"My best friend gave me the best advice
He said each day's a gift and not a given right
Leave no stone unturned, leave your
fears behind

And try to take the path less travelled by
That first step you take is the longest stride

Against the grain should be a way of life
What's worth the prize is always
worth the fight
Every second counts 'cause there's no second try
So live like you'll never live it twice
Don't take the free ride in your own life."

Refusing to let precious moments pass by is very challenging. However, we would be wise to keep in mind that life is too precious to waste on things that don't matter in the long run. Perhaps these final words from Dawna Markova could inspire us to make godly choices from now on.

"I will not die an unlived life.
I will not live in fear
Of falling or catching fire.
I choose to inhabit my days,
To allow my living to open me
To make me less afraid,
More accessible,
To loosen my heart
Until it becomes a wing,
A torch, a promise.
I choose to risk my significance;
To live.
So that which came to me as seed
Goes to the next as blossom,
And that which came to me as blossom,
Goes on as fruit."

May you refuse to let this moment pass!

May you 'Seize the Day!'

May you live every breath for God!

May you do all of this starting NOW!

www.livingingrace.co.za

References

1. From the movie *Dead Poets Society*, 1989.
2. Mark Twain, www.thinkexist.com.
3. W. M. Lewis, www.quotegarden.com.
4. Epictetus, Stoic Philosopher, 55 – 135AD, www.wikipedia.org/wiki/Epictetus.
5. Horace, www.flacc.us/flaccus.html.
6. Mark Twain, www.quotationsbook.com.
7. Theodor Seuss Geisel (1904-1991) (a.k.a. Dr. Seuss), was a famous American writer and cartoonist. www.wikiquote.org/wiki/Dr._Seuss
8. Melody Green, 1989, *No Compromise: the life story of Keith Green*, Thomas Nelson Inc.
9. Jerry Foster, 2004, *Life Focus: Achieving a life of purpose and influence*, Revell, Michigan.
10. Mother Teresa of Calcutta (1910-1997), www.dailycelebrations.com/kind.html.
11. David Brin (1950-), www.perfectapology.com/apology-quotes.html.
12. Leonard Sweet, 2001, *Carpe Manana*, Zondervan, Michigan.
13. The song was on Mike and the Mechanic's album, *The Living Years* (1988).
14. Christopher Morley, (1890-1957) - American journalist, novelist, essayist and poet.
15. Paul Coelho, www.saidwhat.co.uk
16. Steve Mariucci (1955-). Coach of the San Francisco 49ers and most recently the Detroit Lions.
17. Thomas à Kempis, 1983, *The Imitation of Christ: A reading in modern English* (by Bernard Bangley), Highland Books, Glasgow, pg.49.
18. Margaret Storm Jameson quote found in - *Bits and Pieces*, July, 1991, www.sermonillustrations.com.
19. Henry David Thoreau quotes (1817 -1862). American Essayist, Poet and Philosopher, Quoted in the movie, Dead Poet's Society.

20. Sermons by Sergio Milandri, St George's Cathedral, February 2004, www.stgeorgescathedral.com/sermons/sergio-present.html.
21. Nickelback, off the album *Dark Horse*, November 2008.
22. www.allgreatquotes.com/life_quotes.shtml.
23. Vincent Van Gogh (1853-1890), www.brainyquote.com.
24. John Wesley (1703-1791), www.sermonillustrations.com.
25. Dale Carnegie, www.citehr.com/3681-some-quotes.html.
26. Jerry Foster, 2004, *Life Focus: Achieving a life of purpose and influence*, Revell, Michigan.
27. Gutzon Borglum illustration found in *Today in the Word*, January 2, 1993.
28. Anatole France, www.wisdomquotes.com.
29. Michael Johnson, quote found in www.paultreusevens.com/psychology/life-coaching.html.
30. Paul Treu, www.paultreusevens.com/psychology/life-coaching.html.
31. Proverbs 29:18, King James Version.
32. Rabbi Bunim of P'shiskha, www.rishon-rishon.com/archives/2005_01.php, 26 January, 2005.
33. Victor Hugo, www.createthefuture.com/past_quotes.htm
34. Ralph Waldo Emerson, www.wisdomquotes.com/cat_fear.html
35. Les Brown, www.motivational-inspirational-corner.com.
36. George MacDonald, *Unspoken Books*, www.books.google.co.za
37. For more details on her remarkable life, visit www.wikipedia.org/wiki/Wilma_Rudolph.
38. Soren Kierkegaard, www.quotegarden.com/risk.html.
39. Leonard Sweet, 2001, *Carpe Manana*, Zondervan, Michigan.
40. William James, www.quotegarden.com.
41. As recorded by Bryan Mealer, www.bryanmealer.com/new/?p=196
42. Review by Dave Callanan, www.amazon.com.
43. Bill Hybels, *Willow Creek Leadership Summit*, 2009.
44. Gene Edwards, 1991, *The Highest Life*, Tyndale House Publishers, Illinois.
45. John 10:10, *New Living Translation*.

46. Randy Croft, www.sermonillustrations.com.
47. Deuteronomy 30:19, *The Message*, Eugene Peterson.
48. C. S. Lewis, *God in the docks*, pg.52.
49. Jerry Foster, 2004, *Life Focus: Achieving a life of purpose and influence*, Revell, Michigan.
50. Nando Parrado, 2006, *Miracle in the Andes*, Orion, London, pg, 231.
51. John Wesley, www.wesley.nnu.edu.
52. James 4:13-15, *New Living Translation*.
53. Hebrews 4:8, *The Message*.
54. Hebrews 3:12, The Message.
55. 2 Peter 3:11, The Message.
56. Dawn Markova, www.dawnamarkova.com.
57. Nickelback, *If Today was your last day*, November 2008.

www.ingramcontent.com/pod-product-compliance
Lightning Source LLC
Chambersburg PA
CBHW032126050726

47590CB00008B/2976